S0-AAD-941

RECIPES BY GOD

HEAVENLY TASTE
HEALTHY BENEFITS

Easy-To-Make Recipes
That Let You Eat Like an Elephant,
But Look Like a Gazelle

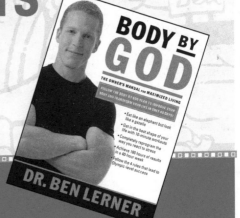

**INSPIRED BY INSIGHTS FROM THE
NEW YORK TIMES BEST-SELLING BOOK**

Recipes by God by Dr. Ben Lerner

Published by Body by God Publishing

A part of Body by God, Incorporated

700 West Vine Street, Suite 201

Kissimmee, Florida 34741

www.thebodybygod.com

International Standard Book Number: 0-97488-1805

Printed in the United States of America

Important Information

Dr. Ben & Body By God do not recommend the use of soy. But for many people—particularly vegetarians—there is no alternative but to use soy. Where soy is used in these recipes, it is used in small quantities.

In view of the complex, individual nature of health and fitness problems, this book, and the ideas, programs, procedures, and suggestions are not intended to replace the advice of trained medical professionals. All matters regarding one's health require medical supervision. A physician should be consulted prior to adopting any program or programs described in this book, or any of the Body By God resources. The contents of this book are based upon the opinions of Dr. Ben. The author and publisher disclaim any liability arising directly or indirectly from the use of this book.

RECIPES BY GOD
HEAVENLY TASTE

Dr. Ben Lerner, is America's Maximized-Living Mentor. His breakthrough strategies for total health and well-being are the foundation to this thriving local practice, which is a center for maximized living, and one of the largest clinics of any kind in the world.

An academic all-American wrestler in college, he has served as physician for the US wrestling teams in six World Team competitions and two Olympiads. At seminars, conferences, and media appearances throughout North America, he shows people how to apply the four laws of Olympic success to achieve optimal health, outrageous happiness, and prosperity. Dr. Ben lives in Celebration, Florida with his wife, Dr. Sheri Lerner. He is the proud father of Skylar and Nicole.

BIOGRAPHY OF THE CO-AUTHOR

Gabriele Bauer is a stay-at-home mom who is devoted to a rewarding and fulfilling career as the mother of five home-schooled children, from infant through age sixteen. Born and raised in Germany, she migrated to the United States when she met her husband of seventeen years, Stan, while he was stationed there in the Army. At the time they met, she didn't speak one word of English, but she knew how to win his heart.

Gabi has always enjoyed creating wonderful meals from scratch; however, before the days of Dr. Ben, the menu was not what the doctor would order. For years she tried to convince her husband, Stan, that they should start eating healthier. He wasn't convinced, stating he would never give up his late night binges of cookies and milk, and that he would never, ever eat oatmeal!

But Stan became increasingly frustrated with his poor health, obesity and low energy. After meeting Dr. Ben, they both learned the incalculable values of healthy eating, and became inspired to dramatically change their lives. Convinced it was time for a change, together they cleaned their cabinets and began eating the Body by God way.

They both knew in order to be successful in this positive change of direction the entire family would need to be on board with the plan. Working with a tight budget, Gabriele set to work, studying, creating, even re-inventing recipes that her family would enjoy. When asked, "what do your kids think of this 'change'?" they simply responded by inviting people over for a meal.

Today, Stan, Gabi, and their children are the picture of health. Stan doesn't get sick, has lost weight, and is a veritable fireball of energy.

Stan and Gabi have shared their recipes with many people over the last few years, and they always hear the same thing: "WOW, we never knew eating this good could be this good!"

Although some items used in these recipes may be more expensive than their "unhealthy" counterpart, you'll find that if you use these on a regular basis, your overall food budget will not increase. In fact, you may find it goes down a bit because you won't be buying all the expensive "junk food." Enjoy!

TABLE OF CONTENTS

Living to Eat

If you're anything like me, eating has always been a part of your cultural, personal, and family makeup. Some of my earliest memories are of food, and food is still the fuel that drives our lives. Holidays, birthdays, special celebrations, Sunday nights, they were—and still are—traditional times around which food revolves.

My family hails from New York City, home to many of the world's culinary delights, including such "health foods" as hot dogs from shiny silver carts, donuts oozing with jelly, and, of course, New York's "world famous" cheesecake.

Not surprisingly, it seemed that everyone in my family and all of our friends' families were slightly "doughy" themselves. Weight problems were constant throughout my childhood, and thus it seemed destined that I, too, would grow up to be fat. Some kids are told they'll take over the family business, others they'll carry on the family name with pride and accomplishment.

As for me, while other kids were being groomed for high school sports, the drama department, Ivy League colleges, and a career in politics, I was being slowly indoctrinated into the world of "husky" clothes and already being fitted for big pants—and by "big" I don't mean "long."

Seeing my destiny spelled out in longer and longer belts and stores with the name "Big & Tall" on the signs, I started to get a little worried. I knew food was a problem, I knew my parents, friends, and relatives weighed too much. I just didn't know what in the world to do about any of it. After all, for years I'd eaten whatever I wanted to whenever I wanted to, just like the rest of my family, without ever once thinking about the consequences.

Sound familiar?

I was raised on the three C's: Cow products, Chemicals, and empty Calories. At the time I only thought there were two major food groups: Fruity Pebbles and pepperoni pizza. If it wasn't loaded with artificial colorings, flavorings, or a list of ingredients even my science teacher couldn't pronounce, I didn't eat it.

I certainly didn't feel unique. I was part of a generation raised on frozen dinners, snacks from 7-11, and a revolutionary way of eating that was spreading across the country as quickly as backsides were spreading across the car seats we were all suddenly eating in: fast food.

Eating to Live

A breakthrough came for me when I actually paid attention to something my eighth-grade health teacher used to say: "Some people eat to live, and some people live to eat." It was like a light bulb went off over my head and someone, somewhere was finally speaking my language.

I thought, "That's me! That's my problem! I live to eat!"

Up until that very moment, I hadn't even realized that we needed food to survive. Like many kids, and adults for that matter, I just thought that food was what I had waiting for me on the breakfast table when I got up, in line at the cafeteria during school, at the dinner table when I got home, and everywhere—and anywhere—in between. I thought food was like TV or organized sports: fun, quick, easy, and temporarily satisfying.

Eighth grade might have been a watershed moment, but the pounds were far from shedding…yet. I still had a long way to go, and though the groundwork had been laid, the foundation was far from solid.

I continued to follow the patterns of my youth throughout my childhood, not changing much about my eating habits and continuing to thoroughly enjoy daily samplings from the 3 C's, not to mention my two favorite food groups.

Slowly, over time I noticed that weight was not the only problem associated with the food I was eating. I succumbed to numerous allergies, illnesses, an overall sense of pain, and a generally nasty disposition that I can now trace directly to the very meaning of my youthful existence: food. But God had a plan, and that plan included me surviving my childhood afflictions and somehow managing to live long enough to attend college. Far from being the picture of youth and vigor as a freshman, though, the joint problems, blood-sugar issues, allergies, and colds that had plagued me all my life were worse than ever.

I'd been a high school wrestler, limping through my seasons by starving myself to meet cruel and unusual weight classes before a match and then going right back to my old eating habits for the rest of the week, and so I chose a college with a good wrestling program in hopes of improving on my injury-hampered high-school career.

Sickness followed me, however, and I spent more time with college trainers and local orthopedists than I ever did in class—or on the mat. It wasn't until I asked an assistant wrestling coach what I could do to prevent such injuries that he told me if I was ever to succeed in wrestling I would have to…change what I ate.

Another light bulb went off and I thought, "What does what I put in my mouth have to do with where I put my arms and legs during a wrestling match? Or how much stamina I have? Or how sore I am after an hour-long practice? Or how often my nose runs or my head aches? Or how much I'm paying in orthopedic bills each semester?"

NEW FOOD FOR A NEW YOU

I knew eating affected weight, but how could food affect my shoulders, back, knees, and immune system? It was another epiphany, another watershed moment, and I wasn't about to let this one go by the wayside for another decade or more.

I decided to heed his advice, and slowly started addressing my eating habits on a daily basis. By observation, by education, by reading, by listening to my body, by being more aware of the food vs. health relationship, I strode past the cereal and bakery sections of the campus cafeteria and wandered into the once foreign land of salad and fruit bars.

Here I met people for whom health was a priority, not a liability. I saw how they didn't come back to their tables lugging trays of donuts and meatloaf, how they weren't wheezing from the exertion of walking from buffet to seat, and how they walked away from the table after they were finished eating as energetic and satisfied as when they entered.

What I found, over time, for it certainly didn't happen overnight, was that if I thought of it as a journey of discovery, I could look at eating differently. I could examine what went on my plate beforehand and not simply regret it afterward.

I learned that feeling bad after a meal was not normal. But I learned that feeling good about what went in my mouth could be. I struggled to enjoy foreign foods like broccoli and carrots and fresh fish, and over time, when I would inevitably stumble and indulge in one of my two favorite food groups, I actually felt ... bad.

Fast forward to today. I know that, like a recovering alcoholic, my battles with food are far from over. In fact, I am not sure I will ever fully recover from the "live to eat" psychology. While many people wake up and consider what they are going to do for the day, I still oftentimes wake up and think less about what I am going to do during the day and more about what I am going to eat during the day. Just as I started doing in college, the trick has been not to give up loving to eat, but to get better at choosing what I eat.

Food by God vs. Food by Man

That's what this cookbook is all about. It is not intended to be the only food you eat. Instead, it is intended to introduce you to the kinds of foods to eat, when to eat them, and how to combine them so that you can feel like I do. And by the way, these recipes are delicious. And my first step was learning that there are still two main "food groups," but now I know that they are very different from pizza and cereal.

Now I'm going to be referring to two food groups: Food by God and Food by Man.

When God developed the body, He specifically created certain foods for its use. These are not foods that come pre-packaged and flash-frozen, are sold over the convenience store counter, or handed to you through a drive-thru window, but foods that grow and exist in nature.

They are, quite literally, "Food by God." Whenever the world gets me down and I begin to question my faith in God, I think of the sheer perfection that went into creating Food by God. For not only has God built into His foods everything that is necessary, but he created them in just the right amounts and in the perfect balance needed, for proper digestion, distribution, and elimination of nutrients.

Food by God is packed with living vitamins, minerals, water, fiber, and the enzymes needed to digest the food itself. When you take in Food by God in its natural state, the digestive system will easily break it down, dispense the nutrients to body cells, and quickly eliminate leftover toxins and by-products.

"Food by Man," on the other hand, is food that is created or altered by man. Designed in laboratories, packed for your convenience, zapped with photons, grown in labs, and filled with preservatives so that you can rip it open a year after purchase and nuke it to perfection. Like the flashy packages and containers they come in, Food by Man lacks life or any truly usable vitamins, minerals, or other nutrients. Anything that is devoid of nutrition or life is unlikely to be able to sustain life.

The farther away you get from eating the foods God specifically created for the BBG, or the farther these foods are from their natural form, the less efficiently the digestive system can break them down—if at all.

Food by Man is almost all indigestible. Because these foods cannot pass through the digestive system quickly and cannot be broken down well, they will linger inside your body. This will block the processing of other nutrients, rob you of power, contaminate your organs, create excess fat storage, affect your mood, and contribute to every type of symptom and disease known to humankind.

Not surprisingly, then, this cookbook focuses on eating Food by God and weeding out Food by Man. Naturally, you will be tempted to substitute Food by Man where it seems most natural. This is understandable, if ill-advised.

The important thing is to use these recipes. If you do substitute the first time you use a recipe, try following it to the letter the next time. Finally, do a taste comparison. Which version left you feeling fuller, more satisfied, and slightly, if not a whole lot, healthier?

Chances are, the one made with Food by God will win your vote.

Timing Is Everything

But knowing which foods are designed by God and which are designed by man is not enough. Knowledge is key, but likewise, timing cannot be ignored. By focusing on the right food categories (carbohydrates, proteins, and fats) at the right times of day (morning, afternoon, and evening) you will see miraculous things begin to occur both inside and outside your glorious Body by God.

Eating Food by God is important. However, eating the way God designed you to eat can be of equal or even greater importance. For maximum BBG health and beauty, it is important not only to eat more of what God wants you to eat, but to eat when He wants you to eat it.

Following the recipes in this cookbook, and those in its predecessor, *Body by God: The Owner's Manual for Maximized Living*, is so effective that even if you do not change the foods you eat but just eat them when you are supposed to, you will see remarkable results in how you look and feel.

The recipes contained in this book are all based on the different needs for carbohydrates, protein, and fats the BBG has throughout the day. Different times of the day, naturally, are better for different kinds of foods.

Morning

At the beginning of the day, it has typically been six to twelve hours since your BBG was fueled, and you still have an entire day ahead of you. Therefore, you need a significant amount of energy-and-nutrient-rich foods. God made energy and the most significant amount of nutrients to come from the foods in the carbohydrate category. Because the body has been at rest, there is not a significant need for proteins and vegetables, which God made as your "building and repair" foods. High carbohydrates are always accompanied by a low amount of good fats.

Afternoon

In the afternoon, however, there is now less day ahead of your BBG, and some carbohydrates are still in the system from the morning meal. As a result, there is less need for energy so thus less of a need for carbohydrates. Because the body has been used to a moderate degree, God created you to add a moderate amount of protein and vegetables at this time. Moderate proteins and carbohydrates together are accompanied by low to moderate good fats.

Evening

Finally, during sleep, there is not a need for "energy foods," so the body was not built with the intention of consuming high carbohydrate foods during this time. There has now been an entire day of body use, so God designed the body to require rebuilding and repair proteins in the evening. Additionally, your BBG will be moving into sleep mode. Sleep is the time when you were created to accomplish most of your rebuilding and repair. A high-protein, low-carbohydrate meal can be accompanied by moderate to larger amounts of fats.

Seven Rules for Better Fueling

So, now we know what type of Foods by God to eat, and just as importantly, when to eat them. But we also know that life is not a book, a television program, or a movie. Life is real, life is imperfect, and so are we. How then to utilize this new way of eating in the real world?

Following and sticking to a brand-new way of eating is extremely hard. In some cases, it is impossible. That is why I created the "Rules for Better Fueling" to help people get better at eating over time. As a result of the Rules for Better Fueling, I have achieved results with literally thousands of people who thought they would never be thin or healthy again or who had failed on numerous occasions to eat better.

To reverse this process of poor Eating habits, use the following Rules for Better Fueling:

The Addition Rule

Instead of eliminating the bad, you will add the good. If your daily breakfast consists of diet soda and a candy bar, you don't "shock the system" by giving them up entirely. With the Addition Rule, you simply add an apple to your cola-and-candy-bar breakfast. Don't think how negative it will be. Instead, begin thinking positively and not negatively. With the Addition Rule, you do not take away, you add. Adding an apple adds a significant level of nutritional value to an otherwise entirely nutritionless meal.

Replacement Rule

Many of the junk foods listed above, in their original form, contain harmful ingredients to the BBG, such as preservatives, additives, MSG, and hydrogenated oils. However, today's modern health food and grocery stores offer a variety of substitutes you can buy or make that are similar in form, satisfaction, and taste to these foods. These substitutes come from Foods by God. They are all-natural and at least provide some actual nutrients.

The 10-Point Reduction Rule

On a scale of 1 to 10, if a craving is a 10, it will be hard to resist. On the other hand, if you can get the same craving down to a 7 or 8, you can control cravings some—or most—of the time. If you can get them down even farther, you can almost totally control them. If you can reduce a food craving down below a level 10, such as by drinking decaffeinated tea in the morning instead of coffee, you will have more power over your decisions to consume. For instance, a cup of coffee or two and a donut is a traditional breakfast for BBG own-ers all over the world. The warmth of the coffee, the sweetness of the donut, all serve to produce a Level 10 craving. However, to reduce this higher craving to a much lower one, try herbal tea instead of coffee. Select a soothing herbal tea that sounds appetizing, and add several healthful "extras," such as honey and some rice milk. What will happen to the BBG's internal feeding system is that it will ingest something very similar to coffee. It won't be as good as coffee, it won't result in any of that usual "zip" because it contains no caffeine, but it will seem like coffee—and your craving for coffee and donuts will subside.

The Vacation Food Rule

No matter how satisfying your work, you need an occasional break. The Vacation Food Rule puts a food, a meal, or even a whole day of the less than ideal food choices in as a rule. The idea that "if you crave, you cave" is a myth. Rather than calling it "cheating" when you give in to a craving, eating poorly on occasion is actually part of the BBG Un-Diet plan. Eat badly once in a while, but do not quit the BBG Un-Diet. Crave, but don't cave. Take a short vacation once in a while, but then get back to work. Eventually, this rule will help you enjoy life even without the vacations.

The Food Dress-up Rule

Man-made foods derive their flavor from all the additives, sugars, salts, and fats that also make them less healthy. God-made foods tend to appear less tasty and fulfilling by comparison. In order to make healthy food more palatable to your abused and desensitized taste buds, "dress up" your food with "tricks" like "cool oatmeal," which is really just your standard oatmeal with different healthy items added to dress it up, such as fruits; soy, almond, or rice milk; nuts, cinnamon, granola, Butter Buds, or healthy cereals.

The Stay Full Rule

Consuming regular, healthy meals at appropriate times of the day achieves a proper balance of staying nourished while also staying satisfied. On the other hand, skipping meals and going hungry lead to a practice of becoming "starved" and create the need for eating anything within reach to satisfy the inevitable hunger pangs. To avoid consuming such "junk" food, always stay full throughout the day with good, God food.

The Multiple Feedings Rule

Multiple small-to-medium-size feedings take less energy to digest, burn well, and speed up the metabolism. To achieve ultimate results with the Body by God Un-Diet and all the ways of better fueling, feed four-to-six times a day.

Maximized Living

I know I've thrown a lot at you, but it's important to me that, with this book, you're not just given the recipes to eat better, but also the tools to eat better for a lifetime. In the beginning and throughout the Body by God Program and cookbook, it will always be important to just start progressing from where you are, getting one-percent better for God each day, enjoying wonderful food, and experiencing the maximized living God intends for you.

Dr. Ben Lerner

Breakfast

CAROB MUFFINS

A delicious substitute for chocolate cake. We've served this to over a hundred people and everyone loves them. The oat flour gives these muffins the texture of cupcakes.

Preheat oven to 400°. Line muffin tin with muffin cups. In a bowl, mix all dry ingredients. In a blender, mix all wet ingredients. Add this mixture to the dry ingredients. Fold in the carob chips. Divide mixture evenly into prepared muffin cups. Bake 15 minutes (or until toothpick inserted into the middle of a muffin comes out clean). Remove muffins and place on a rack to cool.

1 cup oat flour*

¾ cup whole wheat flour (finely-sifted)

¼ cup carob powder

1 tablespoon baking powder

2 egg whites or 1 egg

¼ cup honey

3 tablespoons olive oil

1 cup soy, rice, or almond milk

1½ teaspoons pure vanilla extract

²/₃ cup carob chips

*Oat flour: Pour oatmeal into blender and blend on high until you have oat flour.

2

APPLESAUCE MUFFINS

Here is another dreamy treat. A unique blend of spices adds to the specialty of these muffins, while the applesauce makes them perfectly moist.

Preheat oven to 375°. Line eight muffin cups with muffin paper. In a bowl, mix all dry ingredients, excluding raisins. In a blender, mix all wet ingredients. Add this mixture to the dry ingredients. Fold in the raisins. Divide mixture evenly into prepared muffin cups. Bake 20 to 25 minutes. Remove muffins and place on rack to cool.

1 cup whole wheat flour (finely-sifted)

½ cup oat bran

1½ teaspoons baking soda

1 teaspoon ground cinnamon

¼ teaspoon ground cloves

½ teaspoon ground nutmeg

¼ teaspoon ground allspice

¼ cup soy, rice, or almond milk

2 egg whites or 1 egg

1 cup applesauce (unsweetened)

2 tablespoons olive oil

2 teaspoons pure vanilla extract

¼ cup molasses

¼ cup raisins

BLUEBERRY MUFFINS

Who can resist old-fashioned blueberry muffins? And these are healthy!

Preheat oven to 375°. Line eight muffin cups with muffin paper. In a bowl, mix all dry ingredients, excluding the blueberries. In a blender, blend all wet ingredients. Add to the dry ingredients. Fold in the blueberries. Divide mixture evenly into prepared muffin cups. Bake for 20 minutes. Remove muffins and place on rack to cool.

1 cup whole-wheat flour (finely-sifted)

½ cup oat bran

2 teaspoons baking powder

¼ cup honey

2 egg whites or 1 egg

2 tablespoons olive oil

½ cup apple juice

2 teaspoons pure vanilla extract

1 teaspoon lemon juice

1 cup fresh or frozen blueberries

Tip: Make a double batch and freeze half of them for a rainy day. They won't lose their flavor.

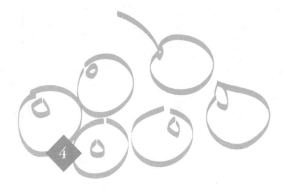

4

CROCK POT OATMEAL

This warm and tasty breakfast is the perfect answer on a cold winter morning when you don't want to get out of bed. Just throw this together the night before and wake up to a house-filling aroma so delightful, you'll jump out of bed.

In a crock-pot, combine all ingredients. Turn on low setting. Cover and cook overnight (6-8 hours).

1½ cups rolled oats

3½ cups water

1 large apple, unpeeled, chopped

¼ cup raisins

3 tablespoons honey (optional)

1½ teaspoons ground cinnamon

1 teaspoon pure vanilla extract

BAKED OATMEAL

Better than oatmeal cookies! My husband would never eat oatmeal until he tasted this warm, crispy treat. This stuff is so good, you'll think you're cheating!

Combine first seven ingredients. Mix well. Spread evenly in a 13-inch x 9-inch x 2-inch baking pan. Bake at 350° for 30-35 minutes. Immediately spoon into bowls. Add milk or fruit if desired.

1½ cups oatmeal

½ cup honey

½ cup soy, rice, or almond milk

¼ cup olive oil

1 teaspoon baking powder

¼ teaspoon sea salt

1 teaspoon pure vanilla extract

Optional:
- warm or cold soy, rice, or almond milk
- fresh fruit for topping

Tip: Dice a fresh apple on this dish for a taste that's out of this world.

6

APPLE OATMEAL

Try this warm, apple-cinnamon alternative to packaged oat-meal products. It's quick, easy and much better for you.

In a sauce pan, combine water and apples. Bring to a boil.

In a small bowl, combine oats and spices. Mix well. Stir into boiling water. Reduce heat to medium-low and cook 5 minutes, stirring frequently. Serve hot. Sprinkle lightly with maple syrup.

2½ cups water

2 large, sweet apples, unpeeled, coarsely shredded

1⅓ cups rolled oats

¼ teaspoon ground cinnamon

¼ teaspoon ground nutmeg

ORANGE OATMEAL

Bring water and orange juice to a boil in
a saucepan. Stir in oats. Cook 5 minutes,
stirring frequently. Remove from heat, cover,
let stand 5 minutes. Serve hot.

½ cup water

1 cup orange juice (unsweetened)

⅔ cup rolled oats

OVERNIGHT OATMEAL

Similar to Crock-Pot Oatmeal, this will give your kids a reason to get up in the morning. They won't be able to resist the delightful aroma or the sweet, delicious taste, and you'll enjoy a hassle-free morning. Don't forget the nuts, they make this recipe irresistible.

In a large crock pot, combine all ingredients. Turn on low setting. Cover and cook overnight (6-8 hours).

1½ cups rolled oats

¼ cup golden raisins

1 large apple (chopped)

3¾ cups water

1½ teaspoons cinnamon

⅛ teaspoon nutmeg

2 tablespoons ground or crushed flaxseeds

1 teaspoon pure vanilla extract

Optional:
· 3 tablespoons honey
· 2 teaspoons chopped almonds or hazelnuts or walnuts

Tip: Serve hot and sprinkle some more chopped nuts on top.

9

PANCAKES

Who said pancakes aren't healthy? These are better tasting—not to mention better for you—than any pancake you've ever had. Velvety texture and extraordinary flavor. Don't forget the Strawberry Syrup (page 116).

In a bowl, mix all dry ingredients. In a blender, blend all wet ingredients, and then add to the dry ingredients. Mix well.

Preheat a non-stick pan, lightly oiled. Drop batter onto pan, using 2 tablespoons for each pancake. Turn pancakes when bubbles form on the top side. Cook until golden brown on both sides. Serve hot.

½ cup oat flour

½ cup whole wheat flour (sifted)

2 teaspoons baking powder

1 tablespoon honey

1 cup soy, rice, or almond milk

1 tablespoon lemon juice

1 tablespoon olive oil

2 egg whites or 1 egg

1 teaspoon pure vanilla extract

Makes 6-8 pancakes

*Oat flour: Pour oatmeal into blender and blend on high until you have oat flour.

OVERNIGHT WAFFLES

With a little preparation the night before, you can enjoy these delectable waffles in the morning. Be sure to make the strawberry syrup (page 116) to pour over these.

Mix all dry ingredients in a bowl. Blend all wet ingredients in a blender, and then add to dry ingredients. Cover and chill overnight.

To prepare: Preheat a well-oiled waffle iron. Batter should be thick. Spoon batter onto hot iron. Close iron and cook 4-6 minutes.

Drizzle lightly with pure maple syrup or top with you favorite fruit topping. (Waffles can be refrigerated or frozen and later reheated or toasted.)

4 cups oatmeal*

¼ cup whole-wheat flour

1 tablespoon plus 1 teaspoon baking powder

2 teaspoons ground cinnamon

4 cups soy, rice, or almond milk

3 tablespoons olive oil

2 teaspoons pure vanilla extract

*Oatmeal= rolled oats

11

HOMEMADE STRAWBERRY JAM

This recipe takes some time, but it will be worth every minute. Spread this on the Homemade Bread (page 13) for a snack everyone will crave.

Put all ingredients in a saucepan. Let mixture come to a boil, then simmer on medium heat for 1 hour, stirring frequently. Pour into jars and refrigerate.

1 cup honey

2 tablespoons fresh lemon juice

1 cup water

16 ounces strawberries, fresh or frozen (cut into small pieces)

5 teaspoons plain gelatin (flavorless)*

*Available in health food stores, made from plants

Tip: Be sure to keep refrigerated.

A simple recipe for extraordinary bread, this bread is a hit wherever we go. Follow these tips to ensure a light, fluffy loaf.

You will need a bread machine for this recipe.

Put wet ingredients into bread machine pan. Add the dry ingredients, adding yeast last. Set on "rapid," "white bread," or "wheat bread" setting.

5/8 cup soy or rice milk

¾ cup water

1½ tablespoons olive oil

3 tablespoons honey

4 cups whole-wheat flour (finely-sifted)

1½ teaspoons sea salt

2½ teaspoons instant yeast

Optional: Add a ¼ cup of sunflower seeds

Tips: Be sure to sift the flour well beforehand using a very fine sifter. Also, the tablespoons of honey and olive oil should be generous.

Be sure to add the yeast last, either using the yeast dispenser (if your machine is so equipped) or by making a small crater at the top of the dry ingredients once they are in the bread machine pan.

OAT BISCUITS

These won't last a minute after they come out of the oven. Top these flavorful, flaky biscuits with honey or our Homemade Strawberry Jam (page 12).

Preheat oven to 450°. Lightly oil baking sheet. In a bowl, mix all dry ingredients. Add oil mix with a fork or pastry blender, until mixture resembles coarse crumbs. Add milk. Stir until moistened. Place dough on floured surface and knead a few times, until dough holds together in a ball. Place a sheet of wax paper over dough and roll to 1/4-inch thick. Remove wax paper and fold dough in half (now 1/2-inch thick). Using a 3-inch biscuit cutter (or a glass) cut dough into 10 biscuits. Place on prepared baking sheet. Bake 10 minutes or until bottom of biscuits are lightly browned. Remove from oven and let cool. Serve warm.

1¾ cups whole-wheat flour (finely-sifted)

¼ cup oat bran

1 tablespoon plus 1 teaspoon baking powder

¼ teaspoon sea salt

4 tablespoons olive oil

¾ cup soy or rice milk

GRANOLA

Don't bother with expensive granola from the store. This recipe can be modified to fit your personal preference. Great for breakfast when you're in a hurry. Also, makes a great take-along snack. Make plenty, it will keep well in an air-tight container.

Preheat oven to 300°. Lightly oil a 10-inch x 15-inch pan. Mix all dry ingredients in a bowl. Blend all wet ingredients in a blender, and then add to the dry ingredients. Mix well. Spread mixture evenly in prepared pan.

Bake 30 to 35 minutes or until light brown, stirring every 10 minutes. Be careful not to burn. Remove from oven and break up any lumps. Cool in pan. Store in container.

2¼ cups oatmeal

¼ cup wheat germ

¼ cup oat bran

¼ cup honey

1½ teaspoons ground cinnamon

½ cup orange juice

2 tablespoons olive oil

1 teaspoon pure vanilla extract

1½ teaspoons almond extract

Optional: Add carob, walnuts, raisins, sunflower seeds or any dry food to the mix.

VEGETABLE OMELET

In a skillet heat olive oil, add mushrooms and zucchini. Cook over medium heat until vegetables are crisply tender (4-5 minutes). Remove from skillet and set aside. In a small bowl stir together remaining omelet ingredients except olive oil and cheese. In same skillet heat 1/2 tablespoon olive oil. Pour egg mixture into skillet. Cook over medium heat lifting with a spatula to allow uncooked portion to flow underneath until omelet is set (3-4 minutes). Place sautéed vegetables and cheese on half of omelet. Gently fold other half of omelet over filling.

1 tablespoon olive oil

1 cup sliced fresh mushrooms

1 cup sliced zucchini

4 eggs, slightly beaten

¼ teaspoon black pepper

3 tablespoons water

½ tablespoon olive oil

½ cup rice mozzarella shredded (optional)

Tip: For even fluffier omelets, add 1/3 cup of water or soymilk to the egg mixture before cooking. Beat thoroughly.

SPINACH & MUSHROOM OMELET

In a skillet sauté the mushrooms, onions, and spinach leaves until tender, remove from skillet. In a small bowl stir together the remaining omelet ingredients except olive oil. In the same skillet, heat olive oil. Pour egg mixture into skillet. Cook over medium heat lifting slightly with spatula to allow uncooked portion to flow underneath, until omelet is set (3-4 minutes). Place sautéed mushrooms and spinach on half of omelet. Gently fold other half of omelet over filling. Serve hot.

½ cup fresh mushrooms

¼ cup onion chopped (about 4 minutes)

1 cup fresh spinach leaves

1 tablespoon olive oil

3-4 eggs, slightly beaten

⅛ teaspoon sea salt

⅛ teaspoon pepper

Tip: For even fluffier omelets, add 1/3 cup of water or soymilk to the egg mixture before cooking. Beat thoroughly.

17

APPLE OAT PUDDING

Preheat oven to 325°. Lightly oil a 1-quart baking pan. In a large bowl, combine oats, baking soda, cinnamon, and nutmeg. Mix well. Add apple, mix. In a small bowl combine the remaining ingredients, Whisk until blended. Add to oat mixture, mix well. Place mixture into prepared pan. Cover lightly with foil. Place prepared pan in a larger pan and pour enough water in the large pan to come halfway up the side of the pan with pudding, Bake 1 hour. Serve warm.

1 cup rolled oats

½ teaspoon baking soda

1 teaspoon ground cinnamon

½ teaspoon ground nutmeg

1 large sweet apple, unpeeled, shredded (1 cup)

3 egg whites

1/3 cup molasses

2/3 cup water

1 tablespoon lemon juice

18

FRUIT OAT PUDDING

Preheat oven to 350°. Lightly oil 1-quart baking pan. In a large bowl, combine all ingredients. Mix well. Place into prepared pan. Bake uncovered for 40 minutes. Serve hot or cold.

1½ cups rolled oats

1¼ cups orange juice

½ cup applesauce

¼ cup raisins

1 teaspoon ground cinnamon

1 teaspoon pure vanilla extract

½ teaspoon almond extract

¼ cup fruit-only raspberry jam

OVERNIGHT MUESLI

Put oats and raisins in a bowl, add the milk, then cover and leave in refrigerator overnight.

Next day, grate the apple and stir in the nuts and honey.

4 tablespoons rolled oats

I tablespoon golden raisins

6 tablespoons milk (almond/rice/soy or oat milk)

I small apple

2 teaspoons chopped almonds or hazelnuts

I teaspoon honey

¼–½ cup of honey (optional)

Optional: Sprinkle the berries on top.

OAT BRAN BREAKFAST TREAT

Line a 4-inch by 8-inch loaf pan with plastic wrap, letting the edges hang over the sides of the pan. Bring the 1 1/2-cups of water to a boil. Add oat bran, stirring briskly with a fork or wire whisk. Cook 3 minutes or until thick, stirring frequently. Remove from heat. In another small saucepan combine cornstarch and 1/4-cup water, stirring until cornstarch is dissolved. Add honey, extracts and cinnamon. Cook over medium heat, stirring until it comes to a boil. Boil, stirring for 1 minute. Add cornstarch mixture, raisins and almonds to oat bran. Mix well. Spoon mixture into prepared pan. Let cool, then cover and leave overnight. To serve, invert mold onto a serving plate, remove plastic wrap and cut into 4 servings. Top with raspberry jam.

1½ cups water

½ cup oat bran

1 tablespoon cornstarch

¼ cup water

2 tablespoons honey

1½ teaspoons pure vanilla extract

¼ teaspoon almond extract

¼ teaspoon ground cinnamon

¼ cup raisins

¼ cup slivered almonds

Raspberry jam to taste

Lunch

Gala

Bel

BROCCOLI & SPINACH OMELET

In a skillet heat the olive oil. Add spinach leaves and broccoli. Cook until crisply tender (4-5 minutes). Remove from skillet and set aside. In a small bowl stir together remaining omelet ingredients except olive oil and cheese. In same skillet heat 1 teaspoon olive oil. Pour egg mixture into skillet. Cook over medium heat lifting slightly with a spatula to allow uncooked portion to flow underneath, until omelet is set (3-4 minutes). Place sautéed vegetables and cheese on half of omelet. Gently fold other half of omelet over filling. Serve hot.

2 tablespoons olive oil

1 cup fresh spinach leaves

1 cup fresh small broccoli florets, cut into small pieces

3 eggs, slightly beaten

¼ teaspoon sea salt

¼ teaspoon pepper

3 tablespoons water

1 teaspoon olive oil

½ cup shredded rice mozzarella cheese (optional)

Tip: For even fluffier omelets, add 1/3 cup of water or soymilk to the egg mixture before cooking. Beat thoroughly.

SPINACH & TOMATO OMELET

In a skillet beat the spinach leaves until tender. Remove from skillet and set aside. In a small bowl stir together the remaining omelet ingredients except olive oil and tomatoes. In the same skillet heat 1 teaspoon olive oil. Pour egg mixture into skillet. Cook over medium heat lifting slightly with a spatula to allow uncooked portion to flow underneath, until omelet is set (3-4 minutes). Place sautéed spinach leaves and chopped tomatoes on half of omelet. Gently fold other half of omelet over filling. Serve hot.

1 teaspoon olive oil

1 cup fresh spinach leaves

3 eggs, slightly beaten

$1/8$ teaspoon sea salt (optional)

$1/8$ teaspoon pepper (optional)

1 large tomato, chopped

Tip: For even fluffier omelets, add 1/3 cup of water or soymilk to the egg mixture before cooking. Beat thoroughly.

25

VEGGIE PAN PIZZA

Preheat oven to 400°. Lightly oil a 10-inch heavy cast iron skillet.

To prepare crust: in a large bowl combine dry ingredients and mix well. Add water and stir. Place dough in prepared skillet. Press in pan. Bake 10 minutes. Remove pan from oven.

To assemble pizza: Combine tomato sauce and spices. Spread evenly over dough, staying 1/2-inch away from edge of pan. Sprinkle cheese and the vegetables evenly over sauce. Bake 15 minutes. Remove from skillet.

Dough:

1 cup whole-wheat flour (finely-sifted)

½ cup oat bran

1 teaspoon baking powder

½ teaspoon sea salt

¾ cup plus 1 tablespoon water

Sauce:

½ cup crushed tomatoes

¼ teaspoon Italian seasoning

Topping:

²/₃ cup shredded rice mozzarella cheese

3 tablespoons each finely chopped onion, mushrooms and green peppers

26

POTATO WEDGES

Make a double or triple batch of these because they will go faster than french fries from your local fast-food restaurant. Dip them in ketchup for a healthy, delicious alternative to America's favorite junk food.

Combine "rice" parmesan cheese, basil, salt, and pepper. Brush cut sides of potato wedges with olive oil, then dip into cheese mixture. Bake uncovered at 400° for 25 minutes.

3½ tablespoons rice parmesan cheese (dairy free)

1 tablespoon dried basil

1 tablespoon freshly-minced parsley

¼ teaspoon salt

¼ teaspoon pepper

1 very large baking potato, cut into wedges (not peeled)

2 teaspoons olive oil in a bowl

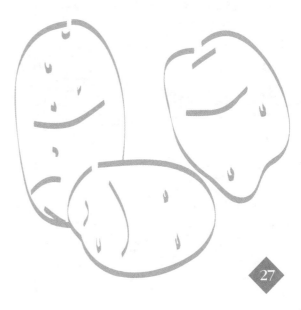

CALYPSO RICE

The perfect Body by God lunch! Very easy, tasty, and filling.

In a saucepan, combine the water, vegetables, and olive oil. Bring to a boil. Add rice. Reduce heat, cover, and let simmer for 20 minutes.

3 cups water

1 medium onion

2 celery sticks, thinly chopped

2 medium carrots, thinly chopped

1 cup each frozen corn, peas, and cut green beans

1 tablespoon olive oil

1 teaspoon sea salt

½ teaspoon garlic

¼ teaspoon pepper

1½ cups brown rice, uncooked

RICE WITH BEANS

This traditional favorite can be prepared ahead of time, placed in the covered baking dish, and refrigerated until needed. Then just remove cover and bake. The perfect answer for leaving Dad home with the kids on a Saturday while you "escape" for some well deserved time with friends.

Cook the rice according to package directions. Meanwhile in a skillet sauté mushrooms, onions, and peppers in olive oil until crisp tender. Add the beans, 1 cup of shredded cheese, corn, peas, Italian seasoning, salt, and pepper. Stir in rice. Transfer to a 3-quart baking dish. Sprinkle with remaining cheese. Bake uncovered at 350° for 30-35 minutes.

1¾ cups shredded rice mozzarella cheese

6 ounces cooked brown or wild rice

1½ cups sliced fresh mushrooms

½ cup chopped onions

½ cup chopped green peppers

½ cup chopped sweet red peppers

1 tablespoon olive oil

15 ounces (1½ cups) black beans, cooked, drained

½ cup frozen corn

½ cup frozen peas

2 teaspoons Italian seasoning

Sea salt and pepper to taste

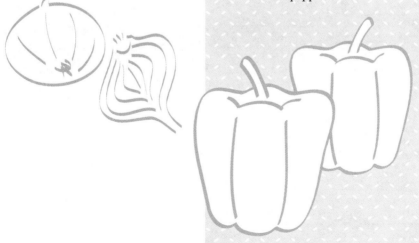

WILD RICE

Your family will go "wild" over this flavorful dish.

Put lentils in a saucepan with the bay leaf and cover generously with water. Bring to boil and simmer 25 minutes. Drain well. Steam broccoli until tender, drain. Whisk together the oil, lemon juice, garlic, salt, and pepper. Pour over hot lentils and mix well. Stir in mint, parsley, broccoli, tomatoes and mozzarella mix well. Serve over cooked wild rice.

1 cup wild rice, cooked

2 tomatoes, diced

¾ cup small broccoli florets

1⅓ cups green lentils

½ cup rice mozzarella shredded

1 bay leaf

2 tablespoons olive oil

2 tablespoons lemon juice

1 minced garlic

2 tablespoons chopped mint

1 tablespoon parsley, chopped

½ teaspoon sea salt

¼ teaspoon pepper

Tip: Lentils can also be soaked overnight to save time.

MEXICAN RICE

A very quick and easy meal, a bit on the spicy side.

Cook rice. Add seasoning mix. Mix well. Fold in tomatoes and black olives.

1 cup brown rice, cooked

1 package Mexican rice seasoning*

2 tomatoes, diced

½ cup black olives, sliced

*Organic mixes without unnecessary chemicals and preservatives, such as Bearitos® brand, can be found in your local health food store.

Tip: Melt some shredded rice mozzarella over this dish, then serve with all natural, organic yellow-corn tortilla chips. (Found in the health food store.)

31

OVEN BAKED POTATOES

Easy and quick to make, but oh-so-very tasty.

Place potatoes in Ziplock bag. Combine the remaining ingredients. Add to potatoes and shake to coat.

Pour potatoes onto baking pan. Bake uncovered at 375° for 40-50 minutes.

12 medium potatoes, peeled and cubed

¼ cup rice parmesan cheese (dairy-free)

2 teaspoons sea salt

1 teaspoon garlic powder

1 teaspoon paprika

½ teaspoon pepper

¼ cup olive oil

SPINACH LASAGNA

We served this dish and no one knew it had tofu instead of ricotta. Everyone loved it!

Preheat oven to 375°. Drain all moisture from tofu. Crumble into mixing bowl, seasoning with a dash of sea salt and pepper and set aside. Mix crushed tomatoes with Italian seasoning, sea salt, pepper, and honey. Place I cup of tomato sauce into the bottom of the baking dish. Add a layer of noodles, followed by I/2 cup of tofu crumbles. Add I cup of spinach leaves over tofu. Add a layer of mozzarella slices. Repeat layers, starting with sauce again, until the pan is full. Press layers down. Press any remaining sauce over the top. Cover with foil and bake for 35 minutes.

I pound firm tofu

4-5 ounces cooked lasagna noodles (whole-wheat or rice flour)

5 ounces fresh spinach leaves

8 slices rice mozzarella cheese (dairy-free)

4 large tomatoes (cubed and crushed in blender)

I tablespoon Italian seasoning

I teaspoon sea salt

I teaspoon pepper

I teaspoon honey

SPLENDID SPAGHETTI

Everybody loves spaghetti and this Body By God recipe will more than satisfy.

Cook spaghetti and drain.

Mix crushed tomatoes with seasonings in a bowl. Brown veggie ground round in a saucepan. Add tomato sauce. Heat thoroughly. Serve over spaghetti.

1 box whole-wheat spaghetti

6 large tomatoes, crushed in a blender

3 tablespoons Italian seasoning

1½ teaspoons sea salt

¼ teaspoon pepper

1 tablespoon honey

½ pound soy browned ground beef substitute*

*Can be found at your local grocer or health food store. We recommend Yves® Veggie Cuisine brand Ground Round.

Tip: To add flavor to the "veggie" ground, sauté with onions, mushrooms or both.

34

VEGGIE SANDWICHES

A great inexpensive alternative to lunch or deli meats. Our kids love these.

Spread mayonnaise substitute onto slices of bread. Top with tomato and cucumber slices. Sprinkle with sea salt and pepper to your liking.

1 loaf of whole-wheat bread, sliced

Tomatoes, sliced to taste

Cucumbers, sliced to taste

Dairy-free mayonnaise substitute* to taste

Sea salt to taste

Pepper to taste

*For the best-tasting mayonnaise alternative, we recommend those made with grape-seed oil, such as Vegenaise® brand.

Tip: Add a slice of rice/soy cheese.

ZUCCHINI BOATS

Impress your friends with this beautiful and delicious meal. The presentation of these makes them look and taste like a real gourmet feast.

Trim the ends of the zucchini. Cut in half lengthwise. Scoop out pulp, leaving a ¹/₂-inch shell. Finely chop pulp. In a skillet, cook ground turkey, zucchini pulp, onion, mushrooms, and peppers until meat is brown, drain. Remove from heat. Add ¹/₂ cup "rice" cheese, ketchup, sea salt, and pepper. Mix well. Spoon into the zucchini shells.

Place in a greased 13 x 9 x 2-inch baking pan. Sprinkle with remaining cheese. Bake uncovered at 350° for 30 minutes.

2 medium zucchinis

¾ pound ground turkey

1 small onion, chopped

½ cup sliced fresh mushrooms

½ cup chopped sweet red peppers

½ cup chopped green peppers

1 cup rice cheese shredded

2 tablespoons ketchup

½ teaspoon sea salt

¼ teaspoon pepper

Tip: Serve with the Creamy Veggie Dip on page 113

36

TUNA SALAD IN A PITA

In a large bowl, add mayonnaise substitute, garlic salt, lemon pepper, tuna, celery, egg, onion, bell pepper, and cucumber. Mix thoroughly. Place generous 1/4 cup filling into pita pocket top with lettuce. Serve.

$1/3$ cup dairy-free mayonnaise substitute*

$1/2$ teaspoon garlic salt

$1/2$ teaspoon lemon pepper

6 ounces white tuna

$1/4$ chopped celery

I hard-boiled egg, chopped

2 tablespoons finely-chopped green onions

2 tablespoons finely-chopped green peppers

I cup shredded lettuce

2 tablespoons finely-chopped cucumbers

*For the best-tasting mayonnaise alternative, we recommend those made with grape-seed oil, such as Vegenaise® brand.

Tip: Instead of pita bread, try rolling the salad in leaves of fresh Iceberg or Romaine lettuce. Not only are you cutting the carbs, but it tastes delightful and looks pretty too.

ROASTED EGGPLANT SANDWICH

Another nice alternative to meat sandwiches.

Preheat oven to 400°. Place the eggplant pieces in a large colander and sprinkle with sea salt evenly. In a large roasting pan, stir together the shallots, garlic, vinegar, olive oil and pepper. Place the eggplant slices and peppers into the roasting pan and coat evenly. Place in the oven and roast for about 30 minutes, turning once. Serve on a grain roll, topped with feta cheese.

3 pounds eggplant (about 2 large peeled and cut 1/2-inch slices)

Sea salt to taste

3 medium shallots, finely-chopped

1 medium garlic clove, minced

¼ cup red-wine vinegar

⅛ cup extra-virgin olive oil

¼ teaspoon pepper

½ tablespoon fresh basil, finely-chopped

2 red sweet peppers, cut into halves

Add feta cheese to taste

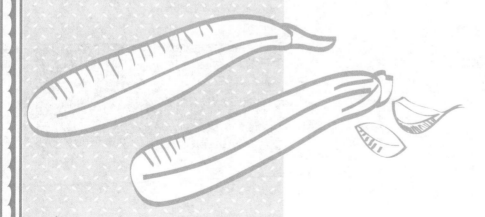

TURKEY BURGER
With Grilled Zucchini and Red Pepper

Serve this colorful entrée at your next pool party. A guaranteed hit.

Season ground turkey with sea salt and pepper, then form into patties. Grill or pan fry until done. In olive oil, sauté zucchini, red peppers, and green onions. Top each turkey patty with sautéed vegetables. Serve with a salad.

1 pound ground turkey
1 zucchini sliced (large)
2 red peppers, cut into strips
2 green onions, chopped
½ tablespoon olive oil

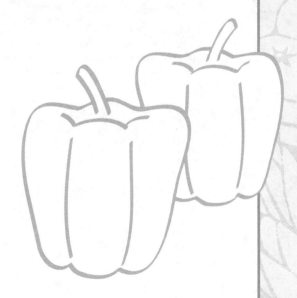

GARDEN TUNA MELT

A healthy twist to an old-fashioned recipe.

Heat oven to 350°. In a medium bowl stir
together celery, mayonnaise substitute and
tuna. Place rolls on cookie sheet. Spread
tuna mixture on rolls. Layer each with one
green pepper ring and one tomato slice.
Bake for 10-12 minutes. Remove from oven.
Top with one slice of rice cheese. Garnish
with green onion. Continue baking for 1-2
minutes or until cheese melts.

¼ cup chopped celery

¼ cup dairy-free mayonnaise substitute*

6½ ounces drained white meat tuna

4 sprouted grain rolls, split and toasted

8 green pepper rings

8 slices ripe tomatoes

8 slices rice cheese (mozzarella)

2 tablespoons sliced green onions

*For the best-tasting mayonnaise alternative,
we recommend those made with grape-seed
oil, such as Vegenaise® brand

40

TURKEY BREAST/VEGETABLE STIR-FRY

A slightly spicy version of an ancient Asian favorite.

**In a small bowl, whisk together the first
eight ingredients until smooth, then set
aside. In a skillet, stir-fry turkey breast
in olive oil for 3-5 minutes. Add
broccoli, cauliflower, onion, carrots
and soy sauce mixture. Cover and cook
for 8 minutes, stirring occasionally.**

I tablespoon cornstarch

I tablespoon honey

¾ teaspoon green ginger

½ teaspoon chili powder

¼ teaspoon garlic powder

¼ teaspoon pepper

½ cup cold water

¼ cup soy sauce

I pound turkey breast, cut into three strips

2 tablespoons olive oil

2 cups cauliflower

I large onion, chopped

I cup sliced carrots

**Tip: For added flair and taste, add
water chestnuts.**

WILD RICE GRILLED VEGETABLES

Trim the stems off the zucchinis and eggplants and carrots cut them length-wise into 1/4 inch-thick slices. Cut plum tomatoes in half, cut peppers in half and spray with olive oil. Grill for 5 minutes on each side. Serve over wild rice.

2 medium zucchinis

2 medium eggplants

6 plum tomatoes

2 medium carrots

2 yellow sweet peppers

Wild rice (as desired)

Dinner

TERIYAKI SALMON

Another great way to serve salmon.

In a Ziplock bag, combine the first 6 ingredients. Mix well. Set aside 1/4 cup for basting and refrigerate. Place the salmon into the Ziplock bag and let marinate for 1 hour in the refrigerator. Drain and discard marinade. Place the salmon on a broiler pan or grill. Broil or grill for 4-5 minutes. Brush with reserved marinade. Turn and broil or grill for 5 more minutes or as desired.

¼ cup olive oil

¼ cup fresh lemon juice

¼ cup soy sauce

1 teaspoon mustard

1 teaspoon ground ginger

¼ teaspoon garlic powder

4 salmon steaks

Tip: Add a slice of grilled pineapple.

GRILLED SALMON WITH ZUCCHINI

A delectable dish for a dinner with friends around the pool.

Marinate salmon in 1 tablespoon olive oil. Baste the salmon on both sides. Grill, turning once. 10 minutes on each side. Spray the vegetables with olive oil, season with sea salt and lemon pepper. Grill on both sides 3-4 minutes each.

2 pounds of salmon or 4 salmon steaks

1 tablespoon olive oil

2 teaspoons lemon pepper

2 red peppers, cut in half

2 yellow peppers, cut in half

4 medium zucchinis, cut into ½-inch wide slices

1 cup broccoli florets

1 cup cauliflower

Tip: Sprinkle the vegetables with paprika on both sides while grilling for added flavor. Serve with the Creamy Veggie Dip on page 113.

45

GRILLED SALMON & ASPARAGUS WITH RED PEPPERS

Sauce: Mix first 8 ingredients in a sauce pan. Cook until shallots are soft (about 3 minutes). Remove from heat. Mix in cilantro.

Baste the salmon on both sides. Grill 10 minutes on each side, turning once and basting frequently with sauce.

1 tablespoon olive oil

2 chopped shallots

¼ cup fresh lemon juice

4 teaspoons honey

¼ teaspoon cayenne pepper

1 tablespoon chopped fresh ginger

¼ cup red-wine vinegar

2 tablespoons soy sauce

2 tablespoons chopped fresh cilantro

2 pounds of salmon or 4 salmon steaks

GROUPER WITH MIXED GREEN SALAD

Try this recipe for a uniquely-wonderful herb flavor. The Lemon Dressing (page 115) with the salad is the perfect compliment to this entrée.

Place grouper fillet in a glass baking dish. Mix all herbs with the mayonnaise substitute, season with sea salt and pepper, if desired, and spread over the grouper fillet. Bake at 325° for 20-25 minutes.

Serve with your favorite salad dressing.

I grouper fillet (large)

I teaspoon fresh chopped parsley

I teaspoon freshly-chopped dill

I teaspoon freshly-chopped basil

I teaspoon freshly-chopped chives

2 teaspoons dairy-free mayonnaise substitute*

Salad

2 cups mixed greens

I cut-up avocado

½ cup cut-up asparagus tips

⅛ cup sesame seeds

*For the best-tasting mayonnaise alternative, we recommend those made with grape-seed oil, such as Vegenaise® brand.

GRILLED SALMON

Tastes best when grilled. Either way, deliciously moist and flaky.

Mix coating ingredients in Ziplock bag. Coat salmon.

Mix seasoning ingredients in Ziplock bag. Shake to mix.

Pour seasoning mixture over salmon or place salmon directly in bag and toss to coat. Refrigerate for 1 hour. Drain and discard marinade. Place salmon skin down on grill over medium heat. Cover and cook for 20 minutes.

1½ pounds fresh salmon

Coating:

½ teaspoon lemon-pepper seasoning

½ teaspoon sea salt

¼ teaspoon garlic powder

Seasoning:

¼ cup honey

3 tablespoons vegetable broth

3 tablespoons soy sauce

3 tablespoons finely-chopped green onions

Option: Place salmon in broiler at 350° for 20 minutes.

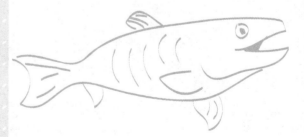

FLOUNDER BAKE

Try this creamy Recipe By God for a fresh alternative to frozen fried fish fillets.

Mix ingredients. Spread mixture over flounder and bake at 350° for 20 minutes.

4 flounder steaks

I cup dairy-free mayonnaise substitute*

I tablespoon freshly-chopped parsley

I tablespoon green onions, thinly-sliced

I tablespoon fresh dill, chopped

½ teaspoon sea salt

¼ teaspoon pepper

*For the best-tasting mayonnaise alternative, we recommend those made with grape-seed oil, such as Vegenaise® brand.

ITALIAN SPINACH SOUP

Best soup recipe ever. People line up to get this savory recipe. It's always in our meal-plan rotation. Add it to yours, you won't regret it.

Meatballs

In a bowl, thoroughly mix all ingredients for meatballs. Shape into 1-inch balls. In microwave, cook them on high for 3-4 minutes, drain.

Soup

In a large pot, add all ingredients for the soup mixture. Add the meatballs and bring to a boil. Simmer uncovered for 10 minutes and serve.

Tip: Our children like it served with shell or elbow pasta.

Meatball mixture

1 egg

½ cup rice parmesan cheese (dairy-free)

1 small onion, chopped

1 teaspoon sea salt

½ teaspoon pepper

1 teaspoon garlic powder

2 pounds ground turkey

Soup mixture

2 quarts vegetable broth*

1 cup chopped spinach

1 teaspoon onion powder

1 tablespoon chopped parsley

1 teaspoon sea salt

½ teaspoon pepper

½ teaspoon garlic powder

*Vegetable broth can be made from scratch by boiling onion, celery, carrots, garlic clove, sea salt, and pepper. (Add other vegetables as desired.) A quicker alternative is to purchase organic vegetable bouillon cubes or organic vegetable broth in the carton—available at your local health food store.

GARDEN SOUP

This zesty, filling soup is another one of our all-time favorites. Quick and easy, yet oh-so flavorful. Our kids love this stuff.

Cook turkey, onion, and garlic over medium heat. Drain.

Add remaining ingredients. Bring to a boil. Simmer uncovered for 30 minutes.

1 pound ground turkey

1 cup chopped onion

4 medium tomatoes, chopped

2 cups frozen corn

2 cups water

3 tablespoons fresh parsley, chopped

3 tablespoons Italian seasoning

1 teaspoon sea salt

½ teaspoon pepper

A classy alternative to regular chicken and vegetable soup.

In a large sauce pan bring chicken broth to a simmer. Add the chicken breast and simmer just until tender and no trace of pink remains, 8-10 minutes. Remove the chicken breast. Transfer to a cutting board and cut into 1-inch cubes. Set aside. Add the onions, broccoli, cauliflower, and chopped spinach to the broth. Simmer for 10 minutes. Add the cubed chicken, parsley, sea salt, and pepper. Simmer 3 more minutes.

6 cups chicken broth

1 skinless, boneless whole-chicken breast

1 yellow onion, finely-diced

½ cup broccoli florets

½ cup cauliflower florets

½ cup chopped spinach

3 tablespoons finely-chopped fresh parsley

Add sea salt and fresh ground pepper to taste

HERBED TURKEY BREAST

A succulent, juicy way to prepare turkey. Serve with one of our fancy vegetable dishes for a perfect holiday meal or anytime.

In a small saucepan, combine the first 7 ingredients. Bring to a boil. Remove from heat. Place turkey in a roasting pan and baste with herb mixture. Bake uncovered at 325° for 1-2 hours, basting every 30 minutes.

Option: Use a rotisserie in place of oven.

¼ cup olive oil

⅛ cup lemon juice

2 tablespoons soy sauce

2 tablespoons finely-chopped green onions

1 tablespoon rubbed sage

2 teaspoons Italian seasoning

¼ teaspoon pepper

1 whole turkey breast with bones (5-6 pounds)

ZUCCHINI CHICKEN DINNER

Quick and easy, yet tasty and different.

In a skillet over medium heat, cook chicken in olive oil until brown. Add onions and garlic. Add pureed tomatoes and seasoning. Simmer uncovered for 5 minutes. Add zucchinis. Cook and stir until crisp-tender.

¾ pound chicken breast, cubed or cut into strips

2 tablespoons olive oil

1 large onion, chopped

2 garlic cloves, minced

2 large tomatoes, puréed in blender

½ teaspoon dried rosemary, crushed

½ teaspoon dried oregano

½ teaspoon sea salt

¼ teaspoon cayenne pepper (optional)

3 medium zucchinis, halved and cut into ¼-½ inch slices

CHICKEN FAJITA STYLE

Although this takes some preplanning, it is well worth it. The chicken comes out so tender and flavorful.

Combine the first 6 ingredients. Divide the mixture between two large Ziplock bags. Add chicken to one and vegetables to the other and turn to coat. Refrigerate for two hours. Drain chicken and vegetables, discarding marinade. In a skillet, sauté chicken for 5 minutes. Remove chicken and keep warm. Sauté vegetables in skillet for three minutes and drain. Spoon chicken into the skillet with the vegetables. Serve.

¾ cup lemon juice

½ cup olive oil

3 garlic cloves, minced

2 teaspoons dried oregano

I teaspoon ground cumin

½ teaspoon pepper

I½ pounds boneless, skinless chicken breast, cut into thin strips

3 small zucchinis, julienne

2 small yellow summer squash, julienne

2 medium green peppers, julienne

2 medium sweet red peppers, julienne

> Tip: Serve with Creamy Veggie Dip on page II3.

*For the best-tasting mayonnaise alternative, we recommend those made with grape-seed oil, such as Vegenaise® brand.

55

VEGETABLE/TURKEY STIR-FRY ON RICE PASTA

In a large skillet, cook turkey, onion and garlic over medium heat until cooked through, then drain. Add bean sprouts, mushrooms, corn and broccoli. Cook for 3-5 minutes. Stir in the soy sauce and ginger. Serve over rice pasta* and toss to coat.

*Pasta made from rice flour found in your local health food store.

1 pound ground turkey

1 large onion

4 garlic cloves, minced

¾ cup bean sprouts

4 ounces sliced mushrooms

1 cup corn, fresh or frozen

1 cup broccoli florets

¼ cup soy sauce

2 teaspoons ground ginger

Tip: Create this tasty recipe vegetarian-style by simply omitting the turkey. It's every bit as good.

56

CHICKEN STIR-FRY OVER RICE PASTA

In skillet, heat 3 tablespoons of broth. Meanwhile, combine the cornstarch, soy sauce, ginger, and remaining broth until smooth and set aside. Add chicken to the skillet. Stir-fry over medium heat until no longer pink. Remove with a slotted spoon and keep warm. Add garlic, carrots, and onion to skillet. Stir-fry for 3 minutes. Add broccoli and peas. Stir-fry for 5 minutes. Stir broth mixture. Add to skillet with the chicken. Cook and stir for 2 minutes. Serve over rice noodles.*

*Noodles made from rice flour found in your local health food store.

2 cups chicken broth

¼ cup cornstarch

3 tablespoons soy sauce

½ teaspoon ground ginger

1 pound boneless skinless chicken breast, cut into ½-inch strips

2 garlic cloves, minced

½ cup thinly-sliced onions

½ cup thinly-sliced carrots

3 cups broccoli florets

1 cup fresh or frozen snow peas

Tip: For added flair and taste, add water chestnuts.

57

BBQ CHICKEN WITH VEGETABLES

Quick, easy, delicious!

In a skillet, brown chicken in olive oil, transfer to an ungreased 13-inch x 9-inch x 2-inch baking dish. Sauté in the skillet onions, green peppers and celery until tender. In a bowl combine the ketchup, water, honey, Worcestershire sauce, salt and pepper. Add sauce to vegetables. Bring to a boil. Pour over chicken. Cover and bake 18-20 minutes at 350°. Sprinkle with corn. Bake 20 minutes longer. Serve with salad.

2 pounds cut-up white meat chicken breast

1 tablespoon olive oil

½ cup chopped onions

½ cup chopped green peppers

½ cup thinly-sliced celery

½ cup ketchup

¼ cup water

1½ tablespoons honey

1½ tablespoons Worcestershire sauce

¼ teaspoon sea salt

⅛ teaspoon pepper

8 ounces frozen corn

TURKEY ROLL

A fancy alternative to meat loaf. The perfect idea for your next covered-dish dinner. Everyone will ask you where you got the recipe.

Mix turkey with sea salt and pepper. Mix filling ingredients in a separate bowl. Place turkey mixture on a piece of heavy-duty foil and press with hands into a 12-inch x 10-inch rectangle. Spoon the filling over the turkey mixture, within one inch of the edge. Roll up (jellyroll style), starting with the short side and peeling foil away while rolling. Seal seams and ends. Place on greased 13-inch x 9-inch x 2-inch baking pan. Bake uncovered at 350° for 1 hour.

1½ pounds ground turkey

1 teaspoon sea salt

¼ teaspoon pepper

Filling:

1½ cups frozen corn

1 egg

¼ cup minced fresh parsley

½ teaspoon sea salt

⅛ teaspoon pepper

MINI MEATLOAF

Serve with your favorite gravy and sautéed mushrooms. No one will know it's not beef. Gravy mixes without all of the unnecessary, unhealthy stuff can be found at your local health food store.

Mix all ingredients well. Roll into 10 equal balls, flattened a little. Fry in pan, turning once.

2 pounds ground turkey

1½ teaspoons sea salt

1 teaspoon pepper

1 teaspoon paprika

1 tablespoon freshly-chopped parsley

1 onion, chopped

1 egg (optional)

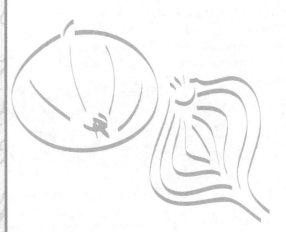

TURKEY SKILLET

This dish is always a huge hit, never any leftovers. It has a Mexican Flair.

Brown meat in a large skillet. Break into small pieces. Add onions, green peppers and red peppers. Cook until vegetables are tender-crisp. Gently stir in sea salt, chili powder, basil, garlic, beans, and corn. Simmer for 5-10 minutes. Stir in some or all of the reserved bean liquid if you want to increase moistness. Gently stir in the olives and parsley. Heat through and serve.

1 pound ground turkey

1 large onion, chopped

1 large green pepper, chopped

1/2 large red pepper, chopped

1 teaspoon sea salt

1 1/2 teaspoons chili powder

1 teaspoon dried basil leaves

2 garlic cloves, minced

1 1/2 cups soaked kidney or black beans

1/2 cup drained reserve liquid (or 8-ounce can organic kidney or black beans)

1 1/2 cups corn (frozen)

1/3 cup sliced black olives

1/4 cup chopped parsley

Tip: If you want to make this a lunchtime meal, substitute the turkey with soy-ground. Serve with bread or all natural, organic yellow-corn tortilla chips that can be found at a health food store.

PIZZA CRUST DOUGH

A Recipe-By-God version of everyone's favorite junk food.

Preheat oven to 400°. Lightly oil a 10-inch heavy cast-iron skillet. In a bowl, combine dry ingredients. Mix well. Add water. Stir until all ingredients are moistened. Place dough in prepared skillet. Press in pan, wetting hands slightly to avoid sticking. Bake ten minutes. Remove pan from oven.

Top with your favorite toppings. Bake 15 minutes at 400°. Serve right from the skillet.

1 cup whole-wheat flour (finely-sifted)

½ cup oat bran

1 teaspoon baking powder

½ teaspoon sea salt

¾ cup plus 1 tablespoon water

GROUND TURKEY WITH VEGETABLES

A colorful, pleasant way to serve meat and vegetables.

In a skillet, cook turkey over medium heat until no longer pink. Drain. Add the zucchinis, carrots, snap peas, onions, green peppers, broccoli and garlic. Cook and stir for 3-4 minutes or until crisp-tender. Add the tomato, salt and cumin. Cook 2 minutes longer.

2 pounds ground white-meat turkey breast

3 medium zucchinis, julienne

4 medium carrots, julienne

1 medium onion, cut into three wedges

¾ cup green peppers, julienne

1 garlic clove, minced

1 medium tomato, cut into wedges

½ cup snap peas

½ cup broccoli

1 teaspoon sea salt

1 teaspoon ground cumin

SLOPPY JOES

Another covered–dish dinner hit.

Brown onion and turkey and drain. In a saucepan, cook green peppers for 2 minutes in a little water, then drain and add to turkey. Add the rest of the ingredients to the turkey mixture. Cook for 1 hour and stir often.

Mix sauce-mix ingredients and add to the boiling Sloppy Joes mixture. Cook another 1/2 hour.

Shred the cabbage and chop the broccoli. Add Vegenaise®, honey and lemon juice and mix well. Refrigerate for ½ hour before serving.

Tip: Prepare this in the crock pot to save time and effort.

1 pound ground turkey

½ cup celery, chopped

⅓ cup green pepper, chopped

⅓ cup onion, chopped

4 medium tomatoes, crushed in blender

½ tablespoon sea salt

⅛ tablespoon pepper

Sauce Mix:

½ cup ketchup

3 teaspoons honey

1 teaspoon mustard

1½ tablespoons vinegar

1 tablespoon Worcestershire sauce

¼ teaspoon garlic powder

Side Dish: Cole Slaw Mix

1 small head of cabbage

1 small bundle of broccoli

¼ cup honey

Juice from 1 freshly-squeezed lemon

1 cup dairy-free mayonnaise substitute*

*For the best-tasting mayonnaise alternative, we recommend those made with grape-seed oil, such as Vegenaise® brand.

VEGETARIAN SPAGHETTI SAUCE

This sauce is a nice vegetarian substitute for meat sauce.

In a large saucepan, sauté red peppers, an onion and garlic in olive oil until tender. Stir in chili powder, cumin, oregano, butternut squash and tomatoes and bring to a boil. Reduce heat, cover and simmer for 10-15 minutes or until squash is tender. Serve over rice spaghetti*. Serve with fresh green salad.

*Spaghetti made from rice flour can be found in your local health food store

I medium sweet red pepper, chopped
I medium onion, chopped
4 garlic cloves, minced
2 tablespoons olive oil
I tablespoon chili powder
I teaspoon ground cumin
I teaspoon dried oregano
2 cups cubed, peeled butternut squash
4 large tomatoes cut up in small pieces

CREAMY CRISPY CHICKEN SALAD

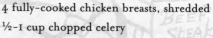

We cannot keep this stuff in the house. It's gone as soon as it's made.

In a large mixing bowl, combine all ingredients. Hand-mix thoroughly with a strong fork. Serve on whole-wheat bread slices or pitas.

4 fully-cooked chicken breasts, shredded
½-1 cup chopped celery
½ cup sliced almonds
½ cup dairy-free mayonnaise substitute*.

*For the best-tasting mayonnaise alternative, we recommend those made with grape-seed oil, such as Vegenaise® brand.

Tip: In a hurry? Look for canned chicken breast in water at your local health food store or grocer. Also, to cut back on the carbs, serve this wrapped in Romaine or Iceburg lettuce leaves instead of bread. Spoon into leaf and roll like a tortilla.

Vegetables

Gala

Be

ROOT VEGETABLES

Great by itself as a "warm salad" or serve with your favorite entrée.

Cook vegetables separately in water until tender. Drain. Combine remaining ingredients, add vegetables, toss and coat.

2 pounds small red potatoes, quartered

1 pound Brussels sprouts, halved

½ pound parsnips, peeled and julienne

½ pound carrots, cut into chunks

½ pound turnips, peeled and cut into chunks

⅓ cup olive oil

2 tablespoons horseradish

2 tablespoons vinegar

2 tablespoons snipped fresh dill

½ teaspoon sea salt

¼ teaspoon pepper

ZUCCHINI SKILLET

A nice compliment to your favorite fish, chicken, or turkey dish.

In a skillet, sauté onion in olive oil. Stir in zucchini, basil, sea salt, and garlic powder. Cook and stir for 5-6 minutes. Sprinkle with tomatoes and olives. Cover and cook for five more minutes.

½ cup chopped onion

3 tablespoons olive oil

3 cups coarsely-shredded zucchinis

2 teaspoons minced fresh basil

½ teaspoon sea salt

⅛ teaspoon garlic powder

1 cup diced fresh tomatoes

2 tablespoons sliced, ripe black olives

SQUASH MEDLEY

In a skillet, heat the olive oil. Add vegetables, garlic, and thyme. Cook and stir until tender, about 15 minutes. Add sea salt and pepper.

3 tablespoons olive oil

1 medium yellow squash, sliced

1 medium zucchini, sliced

¾ pound butternut squash, peeled, seeded, and julienne

1 medium onion, sliced

1 medium green pepper, julienne

1 medium sweet red pepper, julienne

3 garlic cloves, minced

1 tablespoon fresh thyme

¼ teaspoon sea salt

¼ teaspoon pepper

Tip: Serve with the Creamy Veggie Dip on page 113.

SPINACH BAKE

Have trouble getting your kids to eat spinach? You won't when you serve this delicious, creamy side dish. One of our all-time favorites. There's always a battle to make sure everyone gets their fair share. A double batch in our house is never enough.

Drain Spinach. Mix all ingredients. Microwave on high for 3½ minutes. Stir and serve.

16 ounce bag frozen chopped spinach

½ cup dairy-free mayonnaise substitute*

1 tablespoon rice parmesan cheese (dairy-free)

½ teaspoon pepper

¼ teaspoon sea salt

*For the best-tasting mayonnaise alternative, we recommend those made with grape-seed oil, such as Vegenaise® brand.

Tip: Add more Vegenaise® to make this dish creamier.

STEAMED VEGETABLES

A quick, easy idea to serve in a pinch.

Lightly steam vegetables. Season with sea salt, pepper, garlic, and onion powder. Sprinkle with "rice" Parmesan cheese (dairy free).

Any vegetables

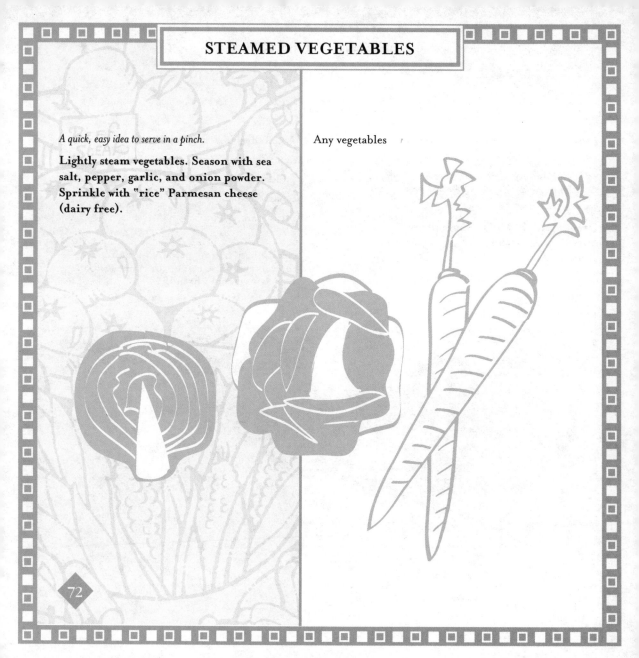

GRILLED VEGETABLES

Try this recipe if you like your vegetables partially cooked.

Spray the vegetables with olive oil, season with sea salt and pepper. Grill on both sides 3-4 minutes each.

2 red peppers, cut in half

2 yellow peppers, cut in half

4 medium zucchinis, cut into ½-inch wide slices

1 cup broccoli florets

1 cup cauliflower

Tip: Serve with the Creamy Veggie Dip on page 113.

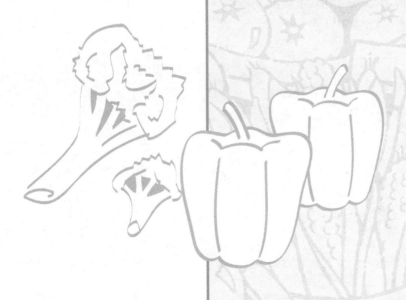

ASPARAGUS WITH RED PEPPER SAUCE

Impress your friends with this fancy gourmet dish. You'll be the talk of the town.

In a large skillet heat oil over medium heat. Add the bell peppers and garlic and cook, stirring occasionally, for about 15 minutes. Remove from heat and let cook slightly. In a large sauce pan of boiling salted water cook asparagus for 5 minutes and drain. In a blender purée the bell peppers until smooth. Stir in vinegar, basil, sea salt. Spoon the red pepper sauce onto a platter and arrange the asparagus on top. Garnish with bell pepper strips and chopped basil.

1 teaspoon olive oil

2 large red bell peppers, coarsely chopped, plus thin strips for garnish

2 cloves garlic, minced

1½ pounds asparagus, diced

2 tablespoons red-wine vinegar

1½ tablespoons chopped fresh basil

½ teaspoon sea salt

¼ teaspoon fresh black pepper

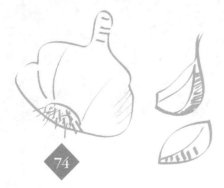

74

A very different way to serve these popular vegetables. Try it, you'll like it.

Sauté the cabbage, celery, carrots, and onions in olive oil until tender. Sprinkle with salt and pepper. Stir in the milk. Cook for 5 minutes. Sprinkle with parsley.

1 cup shredded cabbage

$^1/_3$ cup sliced celery

$^1/_3$ cup carrots, julienne

2 tablespoons chopped onions

2 tablespoons olive oil

½ teaspoon sea salt

¼ teaspoon pepper

3 tablespoons soy or rice milk

Minced fresh parsley

Salads

A colorful, cool side dish to serve with your favorite entrée on a hot summer night.

In a bowl, combine the first five ingredients, set aside. In a saucepan, heat the vinegar, honey, and salt. Remove from heat, stir in olive oil. Pour over vegetables and toss to coat. Cover and refrigerate overnight. Serve Cold.

3 cups cauliflower

2 cups broccoli florets

2 medium carrots, thinly chopped

1 medium zucchini, quartered and thinly chopped

1 medium red onion, julienne

¾ cup vinegar

3 tablespoons honey

½ teaspoon sea salt

2 tablespoons olive oil

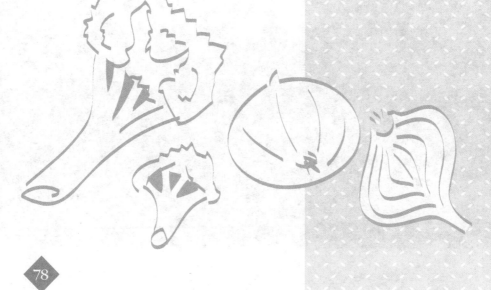

MARINATED TOMATOES

Best tomato dish ever. If you like tomatoes, you'll <u>love</u> this! Next time you have a family gathering at the in-laws, bring this side dish and you'll instantly become the favored relative. They'll want to know where you got the recipe.

Place tomatoes and onions in a bowl. In a shaker, combine the remaining ingredients. Shake well. Pour over tomatoes. Cover and refrigerate for 1 hour.

6 large tomatoes

½ cup thinly-chopped green onions

½ cup olive oil

¼ cup red wine vinegar

¼ cup minced fresh parsley

2 garlic cloves, minced

I teaspoon sea salt

I teaspoon dried thyme

¼ teaspoon ground pepper

BROCCOLI AND CABBAGE SALAD

Another family favorite—your kids will eat cabbage!

Place cut vegetables in a bowl. Pour the dressing over the vegetables. Mix well.

1 small head of cabbage, shredded

1 bundle of fresh broccoli, chopped

½ cup chopped dates (optional)

Dressing:

1 cup dairy-free mayonnaise substitute*

¼ cup honey

Juice from one freshly-squeezed lemon

*For the best-tasting mayonnaise alternative, we recommend those made with grape-seed oil, such as Vegenaise® brand.

> **Tip:** Omit the dates for a fantastic alternative to coleslaw. Serve with Sloppy Joes, page 61.

HARVEST SALAD

Mix dressing ingredients and pour over combined salad ingredients.

Dressing

¼ cup red-wine vinegar

I teaspoon honey

½ teaspoon sea salt

½ teaspoon dill weed

¼ teaspoon pepper

2 tablespoons olive oil

Salad

2 cups sliced cucumbers

I cup red onion, sliced, separated into rings

2 medium, ripe tomatoes, cut into wedges

I cup thinly-sliced radish

I cup avocado, cut into cubes

Tip: Add any of these to your salad for added taste and flair: chopped walnuts or almonds, raisins, shredded rice/soy cheese, olives, leftover sliced herbed turkey breast (see page 53)

TUNA SALAD

A low-carb, quick and easy meal.

Arrange lettuce on plate. Top with tomatoes, cucumbers, olives and tuna. Drizzle Lemon Dressing (page 115) over salad. Sprinkle with parsley.

4 cups shredded lettuce

4 plum tomatoes, sliced

½ cucumber, sliced

2½ ounces sliced olives

12 ounces solid white tuna, chunked

1 tablespoon minced fresh parsley

VEGETABLE CHICKEN SALAD

Mix salad with dressing and add cut-up chicken breast.

Salad

2 cups cauliflower

4 cups torn fresh spinach

1 cup broccoli florets

1 cup sliced cucumbers

2 cups mixed green salad

1 large chicken breast cut into cubes

Dressing

$^1/_3$ cup olive oil

$^1/_3$ cup lemon juice

½ teaspoon sea salt

¼ teaspoon nutmeg

½ teaspoon minced fresh garlic

MAHI-MAHI MIXED GREEN SALAD

The marinade is the secret ingredient here. Excellent flavor.

Mix marinade ingredients well.

Pour over Mahi-Mahi. Cover and refrigerate for 2 hours. Grill for 5-6 minutes on each side. Add Mahi-Mahi to salad ingredients, serve with Lemon Dressing (page 115).

Marinade

2 garlic cloves, minced

1 chopped shallot

6 tablespoons fresh lemon juice

¼ cup olive oil

½ teaspoon sea salt

¼ teaspoon pepper

Salad

4 cups shredded lettuce

4 plum tomatoes, sliced

½ cucumber, sliced

MIXED GREEN SALAD WITH EGG AND RANCH DRESSING

The real treat here is the salad dressing. Use this dressing on any salad. Also makes a great dip for fresh veggies, cold chicken or turkey.

Mix all dry ingredients for dressing. Put in an air-tight container or storage bag to be stored in a cool, dry place. Use this mix any time you need to make a fresh batch of dressing.

Blend 8 ounces dairy-free mayonnaise substitute with 2 tablespoons of ranch dressing dry mix in blender on high. Add water to desired consistency.

Pour over salad and serve.

Salad

2 whole boiled eggs and 2 boiled whites cut into slices

2-4 cups of mixed greens

8-10 green olives

Ranch Dressing Dry Mix

1 cup parsley flakes

½ cup minced onions

¼ onion powder

¼ cup garlic powder

½ teaspoon sea salt (optional)

¼ teaspoon pepper (optional)

⅛ cup basil

8 ounces dairy-free mayonnaise substitute*

*For the best-tasting mayonnaise alternative, we recommend those made with grape-seed oil, such as Vegenaise® brand.

85

CAESAR SALAD

Don't tell Caesar that you know his secret.

Mix dressing ingredients well. Pour over your Caesar salad.

Salad

Dressing

¼ cup red-wine vinegar

1 tablespoon honey

¼ teaspoon sea salt

½ teaspoon pepper

2 tablespoons olive oil

1 tablespoon lemon juice

½ teaspoon minced fresh garlic

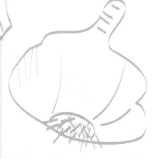

SASSY SALAD

Cilantro makes this salad. Better than any salad you've ever had. This recipe is in high demand wherever we go. Bookmark this page, you will come here often.

Soak black beans overnight in water, rinse and drain. Can be substituted with one 15-ounce can of black beans.

Combine the first 5 ingredients. Mix dressing and pour over vegetables. Toss and coat. Cover and refrigerate for 1 hour before serving.

3 cups frozen corn, thawed

1½ cups black beans

3 medium tomatoes, diced

1 cup chopped green pepper

1 cup chopped sweet red pepper

Dressing:

¼ cup olive oil

2 tablespoons minced fresh cilantro

1 garlic clove, minced

1 teaspoon sea salt

½ teaspoon pepper

Juice from one freshly-squeezed lemon

Tip: Great by itself or served with all natural, organic yellow-corn tortilla chips, which can be found at the health food store.

Snacks

PEANUT RAISIN CLUSTERS

A quick goodie—Between a candy bar and a cookie!

Combine all ingredients in a food processor. When mixture holds together, roll into 24 one-inch balls. Cover and chill.

½ cup oatmeal

½ cup coarsely-chopped peanuts (unsalted)

½ cup raisins or dates

½ cup chopped, mixed dried fruit

½ teaspoon pure vanilla

Tip: You can freeze these for use later.

CANDY BALLS

A yummy treat your whole family will love.

In a bowl, mix all ingredients. Mix well. Divide mixture evenly and roll into 12 balls. Cover and store in refrigerator.

½ cup oatmeal

3 tablespoons peanut butter, smooth or crunchy*

I teaspoon pure vanilla

¼ teaspoon almond extract

2 tablespoons orange juice

I teaspoon honey

2 tablespoons soy, rice, or almond milk

*You can substitute almond or soy butter for peanut butter.

PIE CRUST

Who said eating healthy meant no more pie?

Mix all dry ingredients in a bowl. With a
fork, stir in milk and oil. Work dough into
a ball. Rolling dough between two sheets of
wax paper, form a 12-inch circle. Carefully
remove top sheet of wax paper and insert
crust into pie pan. Fit crust into pan, leaving
a little overhang. Carefully remove remaining wax paper. Bend edges of crust under
and flute dough with fingers or a fork. For
no-bake filling, prick bottom and sides of
crust about 40 times with a fork. Bake crust
in oven for ten minutes at 450°. Cool before
filling.

$^2/_3$ cup oatmeal flour

$^1/_2$ cup whole-wheat flour (finely-sifted)

$^1/_2$ teaspoon baking powder

$^1/_4$ cup plus 1 tablespoon soy or rice milk (ice
cold)

3 tablespoons olive oil

SOFT PRETZELS

These are gone only minutes after they are baked. Our kids love them. Best served fresh and hot, and with mustard for dipping.

You will need a bread machine for this recipe.

Put all wet ingredients (1 cup of water along with the olive oil and honey) in bread machine pan. Add dry ingredients (flour, yeast, salt) to the pan, adding yeast last. Select "dough" setting.

When dough is done, remove from bread pan and place onto an oiled countertop. Gently roll and stretch dough into 12-inch ropes. With a sharp knife, divide dough into four or five equal pieces. Roll each piece into 14-inch ropes. Shape into a pretzel. Set aside pretzels on oiled countertop, cover with a towel and let rise, until doubled in size or about 20 minutes.

Meanwhile, in a large pot, bring 10 cups of water and baking soda to a boil. Reduce heat to a gentle simmer. Preheat oven to 425°. Gently lift pretzels on a slotted spoon into water for 20 seconds. Turn over and repeat for 20 seconds. Remove from water and place on rack, allowing dough to drain. After all are done being soaked, bake on a cookie sheet for 15-20 minutes or until golden brown. Serve warm.

11 cups water

3 cups whole-wheat flour (finely-sifted)

2 tablespoons olive oil

1 tablespoon honey

2 teaspoons instant yeast

1 teaspoon sea salt

2½ tablespoons baking soda

Coarse salt, to taste (optional)

BANANA BREAD

Never throw away those overly-ripe bananas again. With this recipe, you'll buy extra just so you'll have some left that are too ripe to eat plain. Our kids love this recipe.

Preheat oven to 350°. Lightly oil tube pan or bread pan. Mix all dry ingredients in a bowl. Blend all wet ingredients and bananas in a blender. Add to the dry ingredients and mix well. Spoon mixture into prepared pan. Bake 30 minutes. Place pan on rack to cool.

¾ cup oat bran

1¼ cups whole-wheat flour (finely-sifted)

1 teaspoon baking soda

1 teaspoon baking powder

¼ cup chopped walnuts (optional)

½ cup honey

2 tablespoons olive oil

2 egg whites or 1 egg

¼ cup soy, rice, or almond milk

1½ teaspoons pure vanilla extract

2 medium bananas (very ripe)

Tip: Top the slices with a thin layer of non-GMO vegan buttery spread, found in most health food stores and many grocers. We recommend either Earth® Balance or Smart® Balance.

CRANBERRY CRISP

Preheat oven to 350°. Lightly oil a 9-inch pie pan. In a saucepan combine the cranberries, apples and honey. Cool over medium heat, stirring frequently for 5 to 10 minutes, until cranberries pop. Remove from heat, spoon into prepared pan.

To prepare topping:

In a bowl combine oats, finely-sifted flour, cinnamon, and honey. Mix well. Add olive oil and apple juice and mix well. Distribute evenly over cranberry mixture. Bake uncovered 30 minutes or until lightly brown. Serve warm or cold.

2 cups cranberries, fresh or frozen
2 medium apples, unpeeled, chopped (2 cups)
¼ cup honey

Topping:
¾ cup rolled oats
2 tablespoons whole-wheat flour (finely-sifted)
I teaspoon cinnamon
2 tablespoons honey
I tablespoon olive oil
I½ tablespoons apple juice

GRANOLA BARS

Preheat oven to 350°. Lightly oil a baking sheet. Mix all dry ingredients in a bowl. Add oil, honey, vanilla, and almond extract. Mix until all ingredients are moistened. Place mixture on prepared sheet and press into the shape of a rectangle. Wet hands lightly while working mixture. Bake 12 minutes. Remove from oven and cut into 16 bars with a very sharp knife. Separate bars slightly and return to oven for 5 more minutes. Remove from oven and place on wire rack to cool.

$1\frac{1}{2}$ cups rolled oats (oatmeal)

$\frac{1}{4}$ cup oat bran

$\frac{1}{4}$ cup finely-chopped almonds

$\frac{1}{2}$ teaspoon ground cinnamon

2 tablespoons plus 1 teaspoon olive oil

$\frac{1}{3}$ cup honey

$\frac{1}{2}$ teaspoon pure vanilla extract

$\frac{3}{4}$ teaspoon almond extract

Tip: Add any or all of these to make this snack even better: Carob chips, sunflower seeds and/or chopped walnuts.

STRAWBERRY JAM BARS

Preheat oven to 350°. Lightly oil an 8-inch square pan. In a large bowl combine finely-sifted flour, oats, oat bran and baking powder. Mix well.

In another bowl combine honey, oil, apple juice and vanilla. Add to dry mixture and mix well. Set aside 1/2-cup of oat mixture.

Press remaining mixture firmly in the bottom of prepared pan. Spread jam evenly over oat mixture. Drop remaining mixture evenly over jam. Press down lightly into the jam. Bake 20 minutes. Cool on pan, Cut into squares.

¾ cup whole-wheat flour (finely-sifted)

1 cup rolled oats

¼ cup oat bran

½ teaspoon baking powder

¼ cup honey

2 tablespoons olive oil

½ cup apple juice

1 teaspoon pure vanilla extract

⅓ cup fruit-only strawberry jam

APPLE BARS

Preheat oven to 350°. Lightly oil 8-inch square baking pan. In a bowl combine finely-sifted flour, oat bran, baking powder, cinnamon, walnuts and honey. Mix well. In another bowl combine remaining ingredients except apple. Add to dry mixture along with apple. Mix well.

Spread dough into prepared pan. Bake for 35 minutes. Cool in pan. Spread Topping over cooled cake. Cut into bars.

¾ cup whole-wheat flour (finely-sifted)

¼ cup oat bran

1 teaspoon baking powder

1 teaspoon ground cinnamon

3 tablespoons chopped walnuts

¼ cup honey

½ cup apple juice

1½ teaspoons pure vanilla extract

1 tablespoon olive oil

1 large apple, unpeeled, chopped

Topping:
1½ teaspoons honey

¼ teaspoon ground cinnamon

CARROT BARS

Preheat oven to 350°. Lightly oil an 8-inch square pan. In a large bowl combine finely-sifted flour, oat bran, baking soda, baking powder, and spices. Mix well. Add raisins and walnuts.

In a blender, combine remaining ingredients except carrots. Blend. Add to dry ingredients along with carrots. Mix well.

Spoon into prepared pan. Smooth the top. Bake 50 minutes. Cool in pan. Cut into bars.

1 cup whole-wheat flour (finely-sifted)

½ cup oat bran

1 teaspoon baking soda

1 teaspoon baking powder

2 teaspoons ground cinnamon

⅛ teaspoon ground allspice

¼ cup raisins (optional)

3 tablespoons chopped walnuts

1 cup crushed pineapple

2 egg whites

1½ teaspoons pure vanilla extract

½ cup honey

2 cups finely-shredded carrots

BERRY ALMOND OAT BARS

The texture and taste of these bars is similar to baklava, but without the guilt.

Preheat oven to 350°. Lightly oil an 8-inch square pan. In a large bowl combine oats, oat bran and baking powder. Mix well. In another bowl, combine remaining ingredients. Add to oat mixture and mix well. Let stand 10 minutes. Stir mixture and spread into pan. Smooth the top. Bake 35 minutes. Cool in pan. Spread jam evenly over top of cooled cake. Sprinkle with almonds. Cut into bars, serve warm or cold.

2-2½ cups rolled oats

¼ cup oat bran

I teaspoon baking powder

¼ cup honey

I cup apple juice

2 tablespoons olive oil

I teaspoon almond extract

½ teaspoon pure vanilla extract

Topping:

2 tablespoons fruit-only raspberry jam or another berry jam.

2 tablespoons sliced almonds

GINGER SNAPS

These just-sweet-enough cookies go perfectly with a hot cup of your favorite herbal tea.

Preheat oven to 375°. Lightly oil a baking sheet. In large bowl combine finely-sifted flour, oat bran, baking soda and spices and mix well. In a small bowl combine remaining ingredients. Add to dry mixture and mix well. Break off pieces of dough and roll into 25 one-inch balls. Place on prepared baking sheet 1½ inches apart. Place a sheet of wax paper over the cookies and flatten them to 1/4 inch thick, using a rolling pin or bottom of a glass. Carefully remove wax paper. Bake 10-12 minutes. Remove to rack to cool.

¾ cup whole-wheat flour (finely-sifted)

¼ cup oat bran

1 teaspoon baking soda

½ teaspoon ground ginger

¼ teaspoon ground cinnamon

⅛ teaspoon ground cloves

¼ cup molasses

2 tablespoons olive oil

1 teaspoon pure vanilla extract

2 tablespoons water

CAROB CHIP COOKIES

A not-so-sickeningly-sweet alternative to the "bad" cookies. These are great!

Preheat oven to 375° and lightly oil a cookie sheet.

In a bowl mix finely-sifted flour and baking soda. In another bowl mix honey, olive oil, egg whites and vanilla and mix well.

Mix wet ingredients with the dry ones.

Add carob chips and walnuts.

With wet hands roll dough into a desired-size ball, place on cookie sheet. Place a sheet of wax paper over the cookie balls and press down with the bottom of a glass to flatten (1/4-inch thickness) Bake for 10-15 minutes.

2½ cups whole-wheat flour (finely-sifted)

½ teaspoon baking soda

½ cup of honey

¼-½ cup olive oil

2 egg whites or 1 egg

1 teaspoon pure vanilla extract

1 cup carob chips

½ cup chopped walnuts

Tip: Add a 1/2 teaspoon of almond extract to the dough for more flavor.

MOLASSES COOKIES

Preheat oven to 375°. Lightly oil a baking sheet. In large bowl combine finely-sifted flour, oat bran, baking soda and spices and mix well. Add walnuts and raisins. In a small bowl combine remaining ingredients. Add to dry mixture and mix well. Break off pieces of dough and roll into 36 balls. Place on prepared baking sheet. Place a sheet of wax paper over cookies and flatten them to 1/4-inch thick, using a rolling pin or the bottom of a glass. Carefully remove wax paper. Bake 10 to 15 minutes. Remove to wire rack to cool.

1 cup whole-wheat flour (finely-sifted)

½ cup oat bran

1½ teaspoons baking soda

½ teaspoon ground cinnamon

¼ teaspoon ground nutmeg

A pinch of ground allspice

A pinch of ground cloves

3 tablespoons chopped walnuts (optional)

⅓ cup raisins (optional)

3 tablespoons olive oil

¼ cup plus 2 tablespoons molasses

3 tablespoons orange juice

1 teaspoon pure vanilla extract

Preheat oven to 375°. Lightly oil a baking sheet. In large bowl combine finely-sifted flour, oats, baking soda, spices and pecans, and mix well. In a small bowl combine remaining ingredients. Add to dry mixture and mix well. Drop mixture by rounded teaspoonfuls onto baking sheet. Bake 10-15 minutes. Remove to a wire rack to cool.

1 cup whole-wheat flour (finely-sifted)

1 cup rolled oats

½ teaspoon baking soda

½ teaspoon ground cinamon

¼ teaspoon ground nutmeg

3 tablespoons chopped pecans

3 tablespoons olive oil

¼ cup honey

½ cup mashed ripe bananas

1 teaspoon pure vanilla extract

$^1/_8$ cup water

PEANUT OATMEAL COOKIES

In a large bowl combine oats, finely-sifted flour, baking powder and cinnamon. In a small bowl combine remaining ingredients. Add to oat mixture and mix well. Let stand for 10 minutes.

Preheat oven to 375°. Lightly oil a baking sheet. Stir batter once, then drop by level tablespoonfuls onto prepared baking sheet. Bake 15 minutes. Remove to a wire rack to cool.

1½ cups rolled oats

½-¾ cup whole-wheat flour (finely-sifted)

1 teaspoon baking powder

1 teaspoon ground cinnamon

¼ cup honey

¼ cup chopped peanuts (unsalted)

¼ cup raisins

½ cup applesauce

½ cup apple juice

2 tablespoons olive oil

1 teaspoon pure vanilla extract

OATMEAL COOKIES

In a large bowl combine oats, finely-sifted flour, baking powder and cinnamon. In a small bowl combine remaining ingredients. Add to oat mixture and mix well. Let stand for 10 minutes. Preheat oven to 375°. Lightly oil a baking sheet. Stir batter once, then drop by level tablespoonfuls onto prepared baking sheet. Bake 15 minutes. Remove to a wire rack to cool.

1½ cups rolled oats

½-¾ cup whole-wheat flour (finely-sifted)

1 teaspoon baking powder

1 teaspoon ground cinnamon

¼ cup honey

¼ cup chopped almonds or walnuts

¼ cup raisins

½ cup applesauce

½ cup apple juice

2 tablespoons olive oil

1 teaspoon pure vanilla

STRAWBERRY & BANANA DESSERT

All we can say is "out of this world!" Make this and your kids will worship you.

Place all ingredients into a blender or food processor. Blend until very smooth. Chill—it will set. Serve with fresh fruit or as a pie filling.

6 ounces extra-firm tofu

12 ounces silken-firm tofu

2 tablespoons pure maple syrup

2 tablespoons of honey

½ teaspoon of pure vanilla

12 ounces fresh or frozen strawberries

1 large extra-ripe banana

Tip: This goes great with your favorite Body by God cookie.

107

STRAWBERRY ICE CREAM

Pour all ingredients into a blender and blend until smooth (should be very thick).

Pour into container to be frozen for several hours. Very yummy!

16 ounces frozen or fresh strawberries

2 cups of oat/soy/rice/or almond milk

I teaspoon pure vanilla extract

I teaspoon of honey

CAROB BROWNIES

This light, fluffy, cake-like brownie recipe can also be used to make a birthday cake for that special someone.

Preheat oven to 350°. Lightly oil an 8-inch baking pan. Mix all dry ingredients, excluding walnuts and carob chips, in a bowl. Blend all wet ingredients in a blender, and then add to dry ingredients. Mix well. Fold in walnuts and carob chips. Place into prepared pan. Bake 40 minutes. Cool in pan and cut into squares before serving.

¾ cup whole-wheat flour (finely-sifted)

¾ cup oat bran

¼ cup carob powder

I teaspoon baking powder

I teaspoon baking soda

2 egg whites or I egg

½ cup pure maple syrup

3 tablespoons olive oil

½ cup apple juice

½ cup applesauce (unsweetened)

2 teaspoons pure vanilla extract

¼ teaspoon almond extract

2½ tablespoons chopped walnuts

2½ tablespoons carob chips

POUND CAKE

Preheat oven to 350°. Lightly spray a 10-inch tube pan with olive oil. In a large bowl combine finely-sifted flour, oat bran, rolled oats, baking powder, baking soda, cinnamon, nutmeg, and nuts. Mix well. In another bowl combine honey, oil, apple juice, vanilla and eggs. Beat with a fork or whisk until blended. Add to dry ingredients along with an apple, a pear, and raisins. Mix well. Spoon into prepared pan. Bake 45 minutes. Cool in pan 5 minutes and remove to a wire rack to cool.

2 cups whole-wheat flour (finely-sifted)

½ cup oat bran

½ cup rolled oats

2 teaspoons baking powder

1 teaspoon baking soda

2 teaspoons ground cinnamon

1 teaspoon ground nutmeg

¼ cup chopped walnuts

½ cup honey

¼ cup olive oil

1 cup apple juice

1 tablespoon pure vanilla extract

4 egg whites or 3 egg whites plus 1 whole egg

1 large apple, unpeeled, chopped

1 large pear, unpeeled, chopped

½ cup raisins

Sauces

VINAIGRETTE

Mix in blender.

1 shallot, chopped

1 medium garlic clove, minced

1 tablespoon chopped fresh parsley

1 tablespoon chopped fresh basil

1 teaspoon mustard

1 tablespoon fresh lemon juice

3 tablespoons red-wine vinegar

¾ cup olive oil

½ teaspoon sea salt

¼ teaspoon pepper

CREAMY VEGGIE DIP

This dip goes perfectly with any cooked vegetable dish, especially zucchini or squash.

Vigorously mix ingredients. Keep refrigerated. Enjoy!

1 cup dairy-free mayonnaise substitute*

2 teaspoons fresh horseradish

*For the best-tasting mayonnaise alternative, we recommend those made with grape-seed oil, such as Vegenaise® brand.

In a blender, combine all ingredients and blend until smooth. Spoon into a bowl. Cover and chill. Serve cold on sandwiches, crackers, or whole-wheat pita bread.

1 pound can chick peas (garbanzo beans), rinsed or drained (or soak dry beans)

1 tablespoon lemon juice

¼ teaspoon sea salt

2 cloves garlic, minced

LEMON DRESSING

Mix well.

¼ cup red-wine vinegar
1 tablespoon honey
¼ teaspoon sea salt
½ teaspoon pepper
2 tablespoons olive oil
1 tablespoon lemon juice
½ teaspoon minced fresh garlic

HOT STRAWBERRY SYRUP

If using frozen strawberries, make sure that they are thoroughly thawed.

Heat strawberries and honey in saucepan until hot. Do not boil. Pour into blender. Mix for 1 minute on lowest setting. Serve immediately.

16 ounce frozen package or 1 pint of fresh strawberries

2-3 tablespoons honey

Check the Body By God website today to:

- Find the latest information on nutrition, movement, peace management, time management, relationships, and prosperity.
- Sign up for the eNewsletter that will bring the latest in maximized living straight to your mailbox twice a week.
- Ask Dr. Ben questions.
- Learn how you can get Dr. Ben or a Body by God provider in your area to hold a seminar or workshop.
- Find a Body by God practitioner in your area.
- Purchase the finest in nutriceuticals, apparel, and exercise gear.

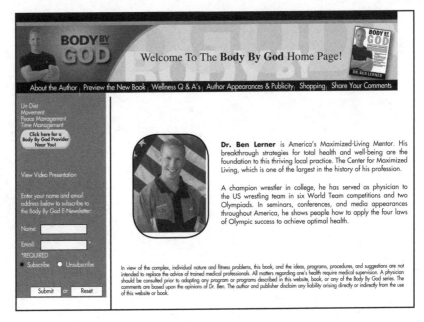

WWW.THEBODYBYGOD.COM